THE ART EXPERIENCE: OIL PAINTING

15th-19th Centuries

THE ART EXPERIENCE: OIL PAINTING

15th-19th Centuries

Leonard Everett Fisher

FRANKLIN WATTS, INC., 1973

*It is much easier to
talk of masterpieces
than to create them.*

Alfred Sisley

Other titles in preparation

Egg Tempera Painting
Fresco Painting
Watercolor Painting
Acrylic Painting
Drawing

See page 57 for Library of Congress
Cataloging in Publication Data
All Rights Reserved

Frontis: Detail of Surrender of Breda, by Diego Velazquez. The Prado Museum, Madrid, Spain.

CONTENTS

Author's Introduction 1
I. The Coming of the Oil Painters 3
II. The Oil Painters 14
Glossary 51
Index 55

Color Plates

Surrender of Breda, Velazquez *ii*
Saint John the Evangelist, Martini *vi*
Portrait of a Man, Titian *4*
The Crucifixion of Saint Peter, Caravaggio *9*
The Arnolfini Marriage, van Eyck *27*
Portrait of a Man, Messina *30*
Young Woman Bather, Rembrandt *35*
Monsieur Rivière, Ingres *38*
The Grand Canal, Venice, Manet *39*
A Sunday Afternoon at the Grande Jatte, Seurat *42*

Opposite page 1: Saint John the Evangelist, by Simone Martini. Barber Institute, Birmingham, England.

AUTHOR'S INTRODUCTION

Long ago a professor of mine at the Yale School of Fine Arts defined painting as the act of applying pigment to a surface. "Art," he insisted—"art, that special something which attracts our attention, excites our senses and invades our spirit—is a matter of opinion. And opinion," he would always add, "is a changing mood."

Having spent the better part of my life in the painting profession as student and workman, I have frequently thought about the simple truth of his definition.

There can be little doubt that the act of painting is indeed the physical process of applying color to a surface. An individual paints if he uses a brush, an air gun, a painting knife, a finger, or a stick to spread some color on a canvas, a wood panel, a plaster or stone wall, or a sheet of metal or paper. The color may take a number of different forms. It can be a watery liquid, an oily paste, a gritty powder, a thin metal leaf or foil, or a stick of "pastel" crayon. All these variations aside, the act of applying color to a surface is the "how" of painting. Anyone who applies such material can be called a painter; he can be a house painter, an automobile painter, or a creator of pictures—an artist.

What matters to some people is the reason that the artist decided to begin painting—the "why" of creative inspiration. And finally, in the end, most people are interested in the visual impression the artist has made by means of applying his color—the "what" of artistic expression. Few people consider the mechanical application itself, the "how" of painting, to be an inseparable part of that special something called art.

Yet, while we painters, past and present, have always had our own ideas about art, I suspect that we are all kindred spirits when it comes to the "how" of our painted creations—the mechanics of our trade. Few experienced artists are willing to form an opinion about painting without considering all the elements, the "whys," the "hows," and the "whats."

All through the history of art, painters have been noticeably preoccupied with either their own method or those of other artists almost as much as they have been concerned with the end result, the final artistic achievement. Technique or method is the road upon which every painter must travel to reach his artistic ideal of making his visions concrete and communicating his inspiration.

As early as 1437, the Italian painter Cennino d'Andrea Cennini commented in his book *Il Libro dell'Arte,* "This is an occupation known as painting which requires imagination and manual skill to make what does not exist appear to exist." And as late as 1915, the modern French painter Claude Monet said, "No one is an artist unless he carries his pictures in his head and is sure of his method."

This, then, is a book that deals with the labor of making paintings rather than with opinions about completed works of art. It is not a how-to-do-it manual. It is not a history book. It is a book that contains certain historical and technical information about one aspect of the painter's craft—oil painting. It is intended to help the reader understand the relationship between the painter's purposes, tools, and renderings.

I have limited the discussion to a period that ends, roughly, with the late 1800's for reasons that have little to do with the exciting artistic explosion of our own modern era. While contemporary painters still employ the oil medium with great skill, the story of twentieth-century art has become more of an adventure in the use of new materials to express rapidly changing ideas about the world — startling but individually creative ideas that seem to belong to no other time but our own. Also, present-day oil painters have not substantially increased the very basic technical knowledge of the oil medium that slowly accumulated during a five-hundred-year period prior to the beginning of the twentieth century. The twentieth century has contributed more in the way of radically changing the appearance of painted pictures than it has in producing important new methods of applying oil paint. Whatever new means have been introduced during the twentieth century does not alter the fact that the fundamental mechanics of applying oil paint still remains firmly rooted in fifteenth-century Flanders, sixteenth-century Italy, and nineteenth-century France. In my judgment, the last great and influential milestone with regard to the relationship of oil painting to the purpose for which it was originally intended — the faithful representation of objects as seen under a light — was reached during the nineteenth century in France. And it is this particular relationship between oil paint and visual realism that is the heart of the discussion that follows.

Finally, this is a book about painting as seen and understood by a practicing craftsman. It is, at best, a small glimpse from within the workshop, the studio, by one who continues to spend his life in such a place, crowded with the light and presence of professional predecessors.

Westport, Connecticut, 1972   *Leonard Everett Fisher*

I. THE COMING OF THE OIL PAINTERS

Oil paint, in its purest form, is color mixed with, or tempered by, any one of a variety of vegetable oils like linseed, poppyseed, or walnut oil. The color, which is ground into a dry powder, is called *pigment*. The basic oil used to form the liquid paint is called the *medium*.

The medium, or *vehicle* as it is sometimes called, has a twofold purpose. First, it acts as a *binder*, or "locking agent," that holds the particles of pigment together either as a damp paste or liquid; second, it behaves as a glue which enables the paste or liquid paint to stick to whatever surface it is applied. The addition of other soluble materials to the basic liquid oil mixture serves either to achieve special effects in the completed painting or to thicken, thin, dilute, or dissolve the oil paint altogether. Whatever is added to the basic mixture of oil and pigment and is miscible with it does not change the broad use of the term "oil painting."

However familiar oil painting seems to us today, the use of the oil medium has enjoyed only a relatively short period of popularity as compared to the long history of man's artistic efforts. Although oil painting was known in the world of the ancient Greeks, Romans, and Chinese, rarely did the artists of that time use oil paint to execute major artistic projects. In fact, the use of oil paint was generally limited to the decoration of such objects as furniture, chariots, or the sails of ships.

Instead, the chief basic fluid used by artists from the beginning of recorded history until about six hundred years ago was water. Water, however, is a nearly worthless painting medium by itself. First, paintings made with nothing more than pigment mixed with water are not waterproof. Such paintings can be washed right off the surface on which they have been painted. Second, such "glueless" paintings can easily be smeared or the color rubbed off with little effort. Third, it is difficult to paint one layer of this glueless, or untempered, paint over another without mixing the layers together and creating an undesired effect. The qualities of this untempered paint are not unlike modern-day schoolroom

Over left: Portrait of a Man, by Titian. National Gallery, London, England. Over right: Typical studies for Portrait of a Man, by Titian (as interpreted by the author).

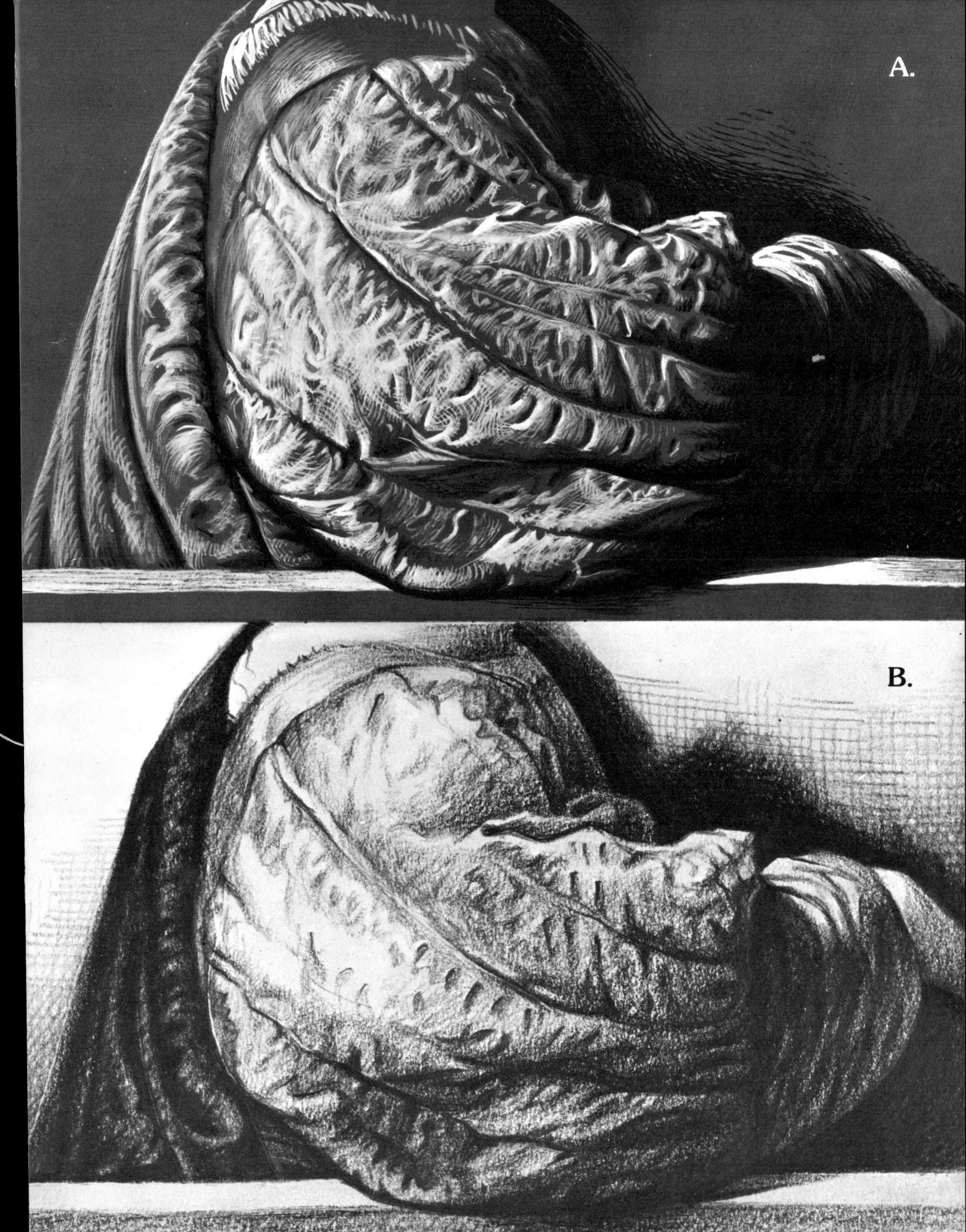

poster paint. Neither contains the elements necessary to make it smear-proof, waterproof, or workable beyond simple areas of flat color.

With all of these disadvantages in mind, painters, in a constant search for new effects, added various binding substances to the basic mixture of pigment and water. They used egg yolk, glair (egg white), casein (dried curd of sour milk), gelatine or glue (flakes of animal bone and skin), or gums taken from certain trees. Each additive was used for a different purpose and each had its own special visual effect.

All of these water-based paintings, no matter what binding was added, had several things in common. They all seemed to be thinly painted throughout, having complete smooth surfaces with no seeming variation in the thickness of the paint. The general *tonality* of these paintings — that is to say, whether they seem light or dark, bright or gloomy — is usually light or high-keyed rather than dark or low-keyed. When looking at such paintings as *Saint John the Evangelist* by the Sienese painter Simone Martini (1284-1344) reproduced opposite page 1, one is struck by the clear light effect. There does not appear to be a variety of deep *tones* in the work.

The *keys* of painting — their light, middle, or dark tonalities can be carefully controlled by the artist. If the artist wishes to evoke sadness, he will work in a low key. A middle key will probably produce a painting of fairly neutral appearance, while a full key containing a wide assortment of bright light and deep darks will produce a dramatic effect. As shown in the diagram on page 7, a high-keyed painting can be produced by never mixing colors darker than the middle tone which is #5 on the chart, or that value of a color halfway between the lightest light and the darkest dark. A low-keyed painting can be produced in a similar manner by eliminating all the light tones above the middle tone. A middle-tone painting can be created by never applying the lightest lights or the darkest darks. A full-keyed painting runs all the way from the lightest lights to the darkest darks in almost equal measure.

Nevertheless, the seeming light appearance of the Martini painting and much of the painting that preceded it over the centuries was not high keyed solely because the artist wished to make it so; nor was it high keyed because that was the absolute limit of the water-based medium. It was a combination of these things. Martini may have thought that his dark tones and deeper accents were indeed deep and strong. But his deeper tones, abundantly used over large areas, would still appear pale before the luminous shadows and darker tones capable of being produced with oil paints. In general, most water-based painting media are

FULL RANGE

II HIGH KEY

III MIDDLE KEY

IV LOW KEY

DIAGRAM OF PAINTING KEYS

PAINTING KEYS—
based on a controlled tonal scale of 9 values from white to black

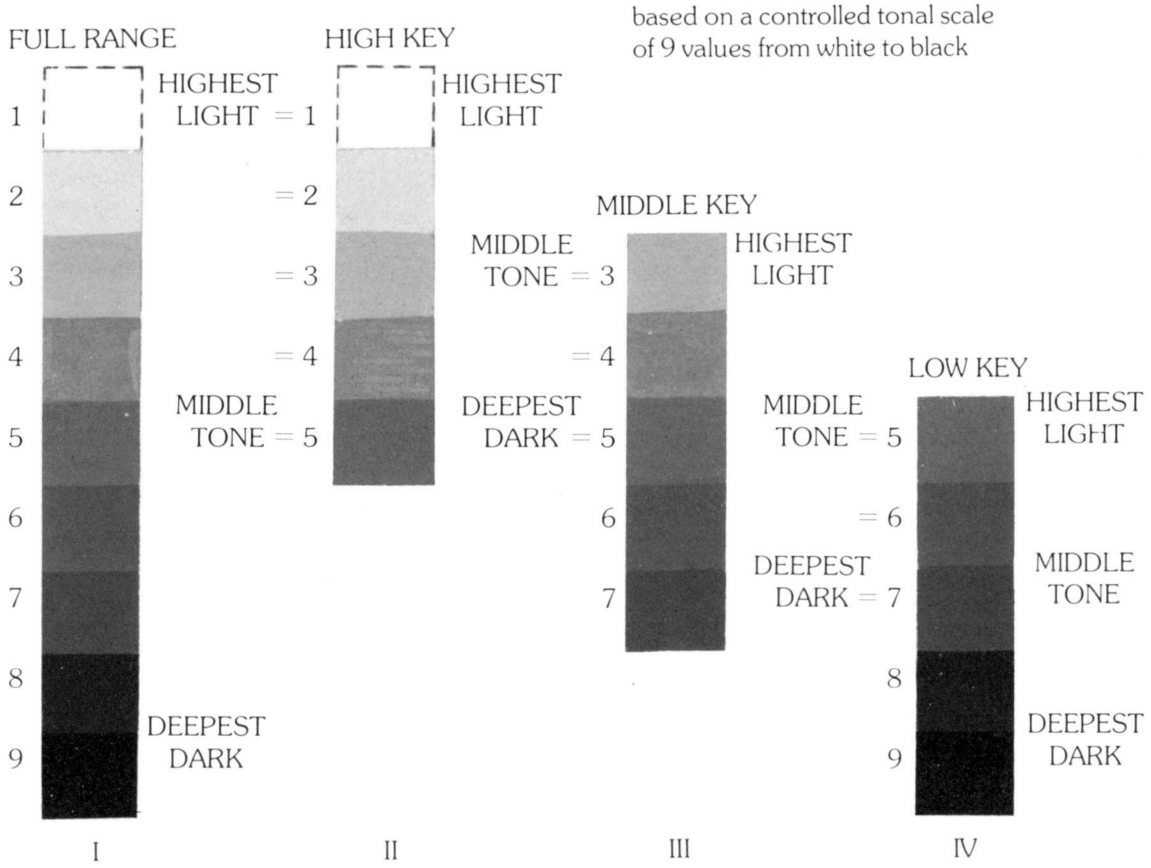

FULL RANGE
1 — HIGHEST LIGHT = 1
2 — = 2
3 — = 3
4 — = 4
5 — MIDDLE TONE = 5
6
7
8
9 — DEEPEST DARK

HIGH KEY
1 — HIGHEST LIGHT
2 — = 2
3 — = 3
4 — = 4
5 — DEEPEST DARK = 5

MIDDLE KEY
3 — HIGHEST LIGHT
4 — = 4
5 — MIDDLE TONE = 5
6
7 — DEEPEST DARK = 7

LOW KEY
5 — HIGHEST LIGHT
6 — = 6
7 — MIDDLE TONE
8
9 — DEEPEST DARK

I II III IV

characteristically higher keyed than the oil medium. There is often a weightless quality in these paintings that is usually not present in oil paintings. While it is a strain upon the water media to make them produce rich dark tones over large areas, it is no strain at all to produce both bright light and rich dark tones over large areas with oil paint.

Another difference between oil paint and some water media with respect to the final appearance of the painting is the linear quality of water-based paints, particularly those that incorporate the yolk of an egg as a binder, like Martini's *Saint John the Evangelist*. That is to say, most of the objects and spaces in the painting were either surrounded by a *structural line* or *descriptive line*, rendered in such a way that every change of *value*, the lightness or darkness of an area, and every change in color, was produced by applying the paint with broad strokes, long strokes, short strokes, strokes that crossed over each other, and closely spaced lines, straight or curved. They were not rendered with smoothly graduated tones or blends of color that eliminated broad brush marks or color edges, an effect easily achieved with oil paint.

A comparison of the Martini *egg tempera* with the oil portrait by French artist Jean Auguste Dominique Ingres (1780-1867), on page 38, reveals this characteristic difference, plainly seen in the execution of the clothing worn by the two figures. Martini, and others like him, painted with narrow strokes or *lines* partly because they wanted to and partly because the water-based medium, in this case, egg tempera, worked better this way and was more readily controlled.

In any event, a painter working in a water-based medium could render a saint, a soldier, or a tree and there could be no doubt as to what these things were meant to be; however, despite their recognizable appearance, these painted objects were lacking in lifelike qualities.

For one thing, objects in nature are not made up of series of lines but of smoothly graduated tones and colors. A blade of grass seen at a distance might appear to be nothing more than a line. Nevertheless, that blade of grass that can be represented in drawing or painting by a single line is a solid form. It has height, width, and depth. It can be held in one's hand. A line is a two-dimensional stroke. That is, it has height — long or short; it has width — narrow or wide; but it has no measurable depth. And since a line has no measurable depth, it cannot be held in one's hand like a blade of grass. A crack in a plaster wall might look like a line to

The Crucifixion of Saint Peter, by Michelangelo Merisi da Caravaggio. Santa Maria del Popolo, Rome, Italy.

some, but then again that crack, however narrow, has height, width, and it has depth. A drawn line on a piece of paper might represent the crack, but the crack, like the distant blade of grass, is not a line. It is three-dimensional. Water-based paints, like egg tempera, did not have the flexibility necessary to recreate or duplicate the nonlinear illusion and structure of nature as nature truly is — without lines.

In addition, all objects found in nature have weight. Even a feather has weight. Also, everything found in nature has a particular surface quality or texture. Human skin, animal fur, plants, clothing, and objects of every description are rough or smooth, hairy or woolly, glassy or grainy. The texture of wool is much different from the texture of glass. And water-based painters, however hard they tried to paint different textures or the illusion of different textures, never really succeeded. It was not their fault as much as it was the limitation of all water-based media. In the end, most of these paintings seemed to be generally without texture. Except for the color differences, the texture of the skin and the texture of the clothing in the Martini painting is identical.

Moreover, everything seen in nature, so far as the artist is concerned, is seen under a light, either a sharp, direct light, or a soft, diffused light. And every object or figure seen under a light, either natural or artificial, must cast a shadow or shadows. And few of the water-based paintings created before the 1300's contained cast shadows. Look again at the Martini painting opposite page 1. There are no shadows cast by the figure or by any part of the figure. The darker tones or shadings are not shadows cast by some solid object. Rather, they are "tones of convenience," dark tones that are rendered without regard for the true or natural illusion that would result from the illumination of a particular light, any light.

The head casts no shadow on the neck. The nose casts no shadow on any part of the face. The arms and clasped hands cast no shadows on the clothed body beneath. The sleeves cast no shadows on the wrists. The collar of the robe casts no shadow on the cloth beneath. And, if Martini had painted the entire figure standing on the ground, he would not have shown the body casting a shadow.

Now, examine the oil portrait by the Venetian Tiziano Vecellio, known as Titian (1477-1576), on page 4. Note how the form of the hair casts a shadow on the face and neck; how the head itself casts a shadow on the neck; or how the bent arm casts a shadow from the elbow upon the stone. Titian "illuminated" the figure in such a way that one can easily imagine that a definite source of light appears to be located in the upper left portion of the painting and somewhere in front of it as well. Given an opportunity, the painter dealing with water-based paints could only approximate the light and shadow construction of nature because of the inflexibility of his media.

These basic "visual" differences between medieval water-based painting and later oil painting — the visibility of narrow brush strokes in one and not the other; the seeming absence of a definite light source in one and not the other; the overall lack of painted textures in one and not the other; the high-keyed, weightless, thinly painted quality of one, and the lower key, heavier, more thickly painted quality of the other — are most important if one is to understand the forces that finally turned painters away from water-based painting in favor of a more widespread use of oil paint.

During the thousands of years of developing civilizations, very few people viewed the function of painting as the duplication of their earthly surroundings. To most people, the world was a temporary place watched over by gods and demons of one kind or another. The world that interested them was not the "momentary" earth they inhabited, but a "hereafter" world, a permanent place that could not be seen or touched in ordinary life but which could only be described by writers and painters. It was this "other world" idea that was the chief subject of the painter during all those thousands of years, whether he was rendering Egyptian tombs or early Christian church altarpieces. Though the manner in which the painters used the water-based media contributed to the somewhat unnatural appearance of the objects and figures in the paintings, it was the physical characteristics of the water-based media themselves that produced the weightless, airless, flatly linear, high-keyed paintings with the desired unearthly look.

Nevertheless, man moved slowly toward a new and different point of view about the world in which he lived and the world of the "hereafter." And it was this awakening, changing attitude that heralded the dawn of a new age — the modern era — and with it, the coming of the oil painters.

Between the fourth century A.D., when the Roman Empire was divided into Rome West and Constantinople East, and the fifteenth century, when faint but stubborn religious protest was heard in the North, Europe was convulsed by endless political and religious turmoil, scientific discovery, and violence. During this period the Roman Empire was destroyed. It was a period of the rise and fall of the power of the Catholic popes, a span of time which saw the medieval era begin under the influence of the spiritual East only to give way to the Renaissance era and the influence of the practical West. The Renaissance, which began during the fifteenth century, was an age of humanism. Humanism was based on the idea that man, not the church, is the center of the universe. The humanists began to delight in the earthly objects surrounding them. To them it was more important to enjoy the smell of fragrant flowers in one's own garden than to worry about whether or not there was any garden at all in the "hereafter." It was more important to study the world as it is than to speculate about another world that no one could really see; it was more important to be joyfully alive than sorrowfully dead. Humanism turned religious emphasis in the West away from the "heavenly hereafter" to the more "worldly now."

Numerous other factors contributed to the growth of the humanist spirit. Scientific experimentation focused man's attention on the operation of natural phenomena, both in the world around him and within himself. The growth of commerce and industry resulted in the rise of cities and a middle class also interested in being represented in the world of art. Changing political forces created different artistic climates in various parts of Europe. The development of a new feeling about art was related to the changing religious, social, and political events of the time.

It was during this long tumultuous period that the artistic or cultural split between the still spiritual East and the more worldly, aggressive West became sharply focused. The Western character had come to demand more objectivity, and more earthly realism in its art, while the Eastern character continued to demand a more subjective, abstract, ornamental art. The old water-based media, while still useful in the East, because there was no need to fully portray the natural appearance of things, no longer served the needs of Western thought. Slowly, Western painters, Flemings, Italians, Dutch, Spanish, and Germans began to explore the new painting medium of oil as a way to achieve the look of worldly realism demanded of their art.

Until this change in attitude had begun to occur — that is, man's increasing interest in himself and in his own living world — he painted his pictures for ceremonial reasons. And in dealing artistically with the awesomeness of the spiritual world, it was not outrageous of him to believe that the spiritual world was bound by a different set of physical laws than those that govern life on this earth. The law of gravity, for example, whether he knew or even understood such a science, had nothing whatever to do with heaven or hell. As such, the artist's imaginative representation of the hereafter was real enough, but less than a lifelike impression found in the everyday world. Thus, it was not really necessary for those early painters to know *atmospheric perspective,* a method for creating airy painted distances. They did not have to know *linear perspective,* a mathematical concept for creating the illusion of distance. They did not have to know how to represent the illusion of light, dark, and cast shadow because these elements of visual reality are governed by specific natural laws peculiar to our earthly existence.

    Because man's attitude toward himself and the world around him was changing, his artistic need for new styles and media was growing. He sought additional knowledge that would enable him to create satisfying representations of the real world. He also needed a painting medium that could create an illusion of earthly atmosphere, space, and convincing human flesh. The popularity of the oil medium arose in conjunction with the changing needs in the world of the artist and those around him.

II.
THE OIL PAINTERS

Oil paint has several characteristics that distinguish it from all other painting media. For one thing, it dries more slowly than any other medium. This can be either a distinct disadvantage for the artist who wants his painting to dry as he works on it, or it can be very advantageous to the artist who wants his painting to remain wet and workable in order to create certain effects. The slow drying time of oil paint makes the medium very plastic. That is to say, whether it is thick or thin, transparent or opaque, it can still be manipulated to create smooth blends of color without lines, or crisp bold areas, without weakening the color *intensity,* or strength, of the color. Oil paint is so flexible that it can be worked over, altered, pushed around, or wiped off in a unique way. Mistakes can easily be corrected. This flexibility gives the artist more freedom of execution, which is unlike the fast-drying egg-water medium that requires absolute discipline of execution and allows little possibility for changes.

Moreover, oil paint can produce the highest lights of the light-keyed water media and the deepest darks of any medium known. The oil painting by Italian artist Michelangelo Merisi da Caravaggio (c. 1573-c. 1609), *The Crucifixion of Saint Peter,* on page 9, clearly demonstrates the wide value range, the assortment of deep darks, middle tones, and bright lights, naturally characteristic of the oil medium.

And finally, a brief comparison of an oil painting with a water-based painting will generally reveal that the overall appearance of the oil is warmer and softer than any other painting medium used before the twentieth century.

Most of these qualities, if not all of them, were first properly appreciated and put to use by the Flemish painters of northern Europe during the fifteenth century. Among these painters were the van Eyck brothers, Hubert (c. 1380-1426) and Jan (c. 1390-1441); Roger Van Der Weyden (c. 1400-64); Hans Memling (c. 1440-94), a German-born citizen of Flanders; and Hugo Van Der Goes (c. 1440-82).

During the Middle Ages, the Flemish painters had devoted their time to the creation of very small works, usually manuscript illuminations, the decoration or illustration of hand-lettered books. These Northern painters were restricted to small works because the churches and public buildings of their locales did not have great wall spaces for mural paintings. For the most part, the Flemings used the egg-water medium since it was most practical for small-scale work. From time to time some of these artists painted larger-sized freestanding altarpieces, paintings created especially for church altars that were executed on wood panels and were in no way part of the structural walls of the building. Some of these Flemish altarpieces appeared to be large-sized miniatures because they were so full of tiny, carefully rendered detail. And it was in these altarpieces that a change in painting media first became noticeable.

Although the fifteenth-century Flemings were more concerned about the events of everyday life than most southern Europeans, they were beginning to be engulfed by a great philosophical movement that focused a large part of its attention upon the earthly world rather than the religious world of the hereafter. The ideas that were influencing the Flemings would soon challenge the authority of the Roman Catholic popes, if not the entire Catholic church, and sweep across northern Europe in bitter protest culminating in one mammoth outcry called the Protestant Reformation.

Many of the Flemish paintings, although religious in content, reflected the growing respect accorded to man and his world. These paintings were devoted more to the surface appearance of an object or figure, however, than to the spiritual significance of these things. The Flemish painters already had an intense interest in copying nature. And by the time the van Eyck brothers arrived on the scene, the precise rendering of every form found in the real world of nature was more important to Flemish painters than anything else in their artistic creations. Now their passion was to paint these forms as naturally as they appeared to the human eye.

The exact ingredients of fifteenth-century Flemish oil paint are not entirely known. But the methods of applying these paints are better known. While the mysterious Flemish oil ingredients had much to do with the final appearance of these enamel-hard, brilliantly colored, jewel-like paintings, so too did the method of applying those ingredients.

The Flemings knew a great deal about the always complicated methods of medieval painting. They were careful craftsmen, having practiced their skills by patiently painting detailed miniatures and manuscript illumination. The controlled clarity of their art was ample evidence of skill that was, indeed, a long time in developing.

The Flemish painters knew about the latest scientific advances unfolding in the art guilds of Florence, Italy, and elsewhere. They were familiar with Italian painting of all types. They had journeyed to Florence and Venice, bringing with them their own ideas about realism. And while they took back to Flanders new ideas and techniques to enrich their own paintings, their work developed along independent lines until the end of the fifteenth century. They also took home with them commissions for work contracted by Florentines. This was a form of trade exchange since Florentine artists had been commissioned time and again by Flemish businessmen to create designs for *tapestries.*

Long aware of the usefulness of oil as a painting medium, the Flemings put the old techniques together with some new ones and achieved in their paintings a clean, sharp realistic effect rarely seen before. These paintings became an artistic bridge between the flat appearance of medieval painting and the rounder, more solid appearance of Renaissance painting. With their "new look" the industrious Flemings were able to compete successfully with Italian painters whose reputations until then had far exceeded their own. For their part, the Italians were astounded by what they saw.

To produce these new "oil" paintings, the Flemings followed, at first, the same preliminary steps used to create the customary egg-tempera paintings—again, pigment ground in water and tempered or mixed with the yolk of an egg, the binding substance. They plastered a wood panel called a *carrier* with seven or eight coats of a warm liquid mixture of white chalk, glue *size,* and water, called *gesso.* The glue size was gelatine shavings melted in warm water. This was the liquid binder that caused the chalk to stick to the surface of the carrier, hence the term glue size. The preparation of fifteenth-century gesso is not unlike the preparation of gesso today.

Present-day painters who prepare their own water-based gesso usually use a powdered chalky material called whiting. The whiting is poured through a flour sifter into a warm solution of gelatine and water until a fine crust appears on the surface of the solution. The whiting-gelatine-water mixture which is somewhat lumpy is then slowly poured through a strainer into a fresh pot. The lumpy parts of the mixture are pushed through the strainer with a stiff brush. The resulting mixture or gesso is the same today as it was in the fifteenth century—a near-white, creamy, warm liquid. This water-based gesso is brushed onto a stiff carrier, such as wood or masonite, rather than a pliant canvas; and it is brushed on in about seven or eight successive layers as each layer dries. There are further, more complicated steps, involving the making and application of gesso. However, the end product is a reasonably hard, somewhat absorbent surface which becomes dead white when perfectly dry.

This surface, called the *ground,* is then sanded absolutely smooth. It was on such a ground that the Flemish painters began their paintings by first preparing a charcoal drawing, usually a line drawing of the design.

The charcoal drawing was either dusted off when completed, leaving a faint impression for the artist to follow, or was secured to the ground after dusting, by brushing on a weak solution of glue size. The solution was not strong enough to be an impenetrable film or a hardening agent that would make the gesso nonabsorbent. The gesso ground remained just hard enough so that the color would not soak into it but would retain its intensity, or a controlled brilliance.

Next, the painter brushed on the all-important *underpainting,* a preliminary *monochromatic,* or one-color, painting. The underpainting together with the smooth white gesso ground had a direct effect on the final appearance of the painting. More than likely, the underpainting was a black ink rendering similar to the black ink rendering on page 26. It was done almost as carefully as the *overpainting* or the final application of color. The deepest darks were done in pure black. The middle tones were painted in with a water diluted black to give a grayish appearance. The lighter areas and some selected middle-tone areas were left untouched and pure white.

The illustration on page 26 shows the typical ink underpainting of a section of the painting on the facing page, *The Arnolfini Marriage,* as the artist Jan van Eyck might have rendered it. Note that the *rendering* of the forms in the underpainting is accomplished with short strokes or lines, rather than with wide, flat "washes" of ink. This use of line to "model" the forms gave the artist better control over the solid or three-dimensional effect he sought. (Also, the linear rendering of the watery ink would be similar to the traditional linear manner in which the next step—a water-base color step—would be handled.)

The underpainting served many and varied purposes. It gave the painter a map of his light and dark tones; it blocked out the dazzling white gesso ground that would tend to come through the thinly painted and translucent dark areas of the final painting; it increased the brilliance and power of the light areas which were thicker and more *opaque;* and it held steady the light, middle, and dark values of the painting as it became older. Most paint, however color-permanent, becomes more transparent with age. This circumstance did not matter so much with the light colors; these were backed up by the pure white ground underneath. It did matter to the dark colors, however. If the dark colors were not underpainted, their increasing transparency, which developed at a faster pace

A.

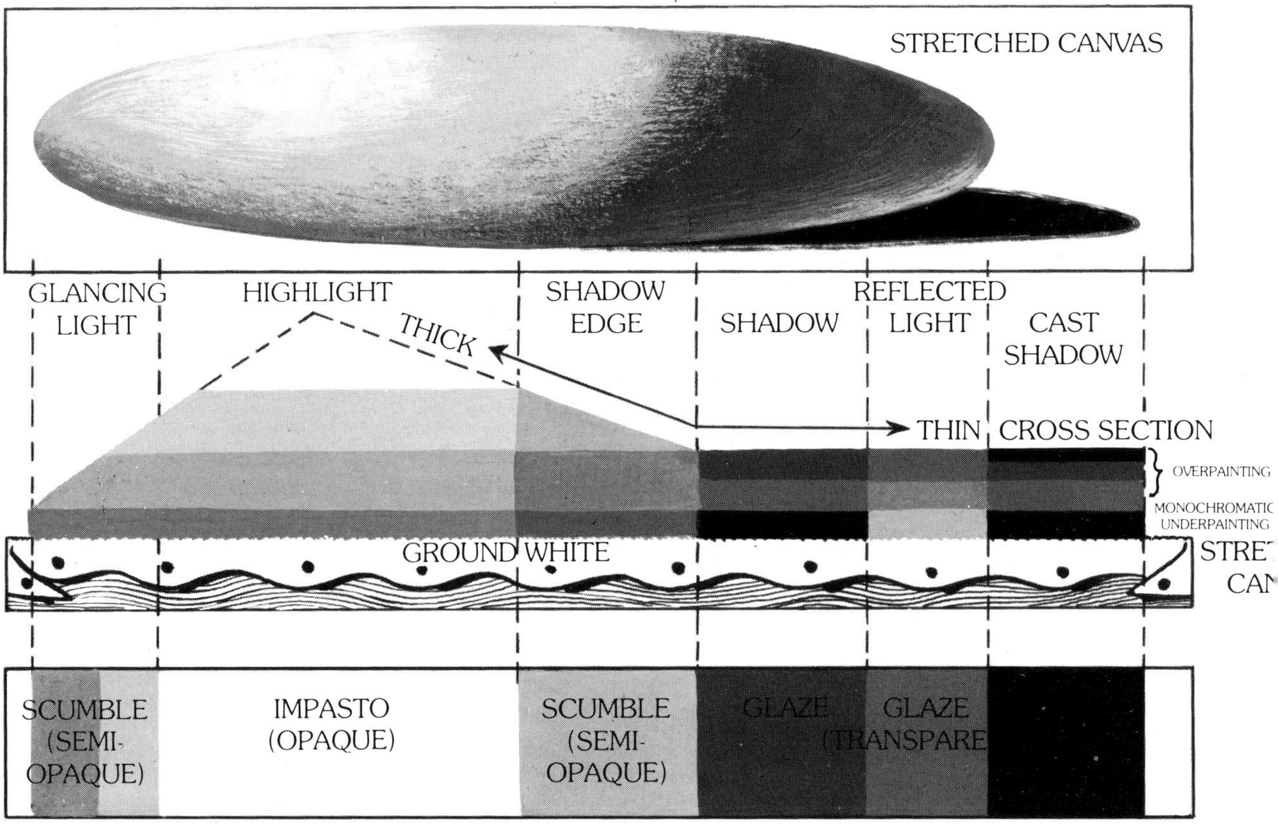

| GLANCING LIGHT | HIGHLIGHT | SHADOW EDGE | SHADOW | REFLECTED LIGHT | CAST SHADOW |

THICK ← → THIN CROSS SECTION

OVERPAINTING
MONOCHROMATIC UNDERPAINTING

GROUND WHITE

STRETCHED CANVAS

| SCUMBLE (SEMI-OPAQUE) | IMPASTO (OPAQUE) | SCUMBLE (SEMI-OPAQUE) | GLAZE | GLAZE (TRANSPARENT) | |

B.

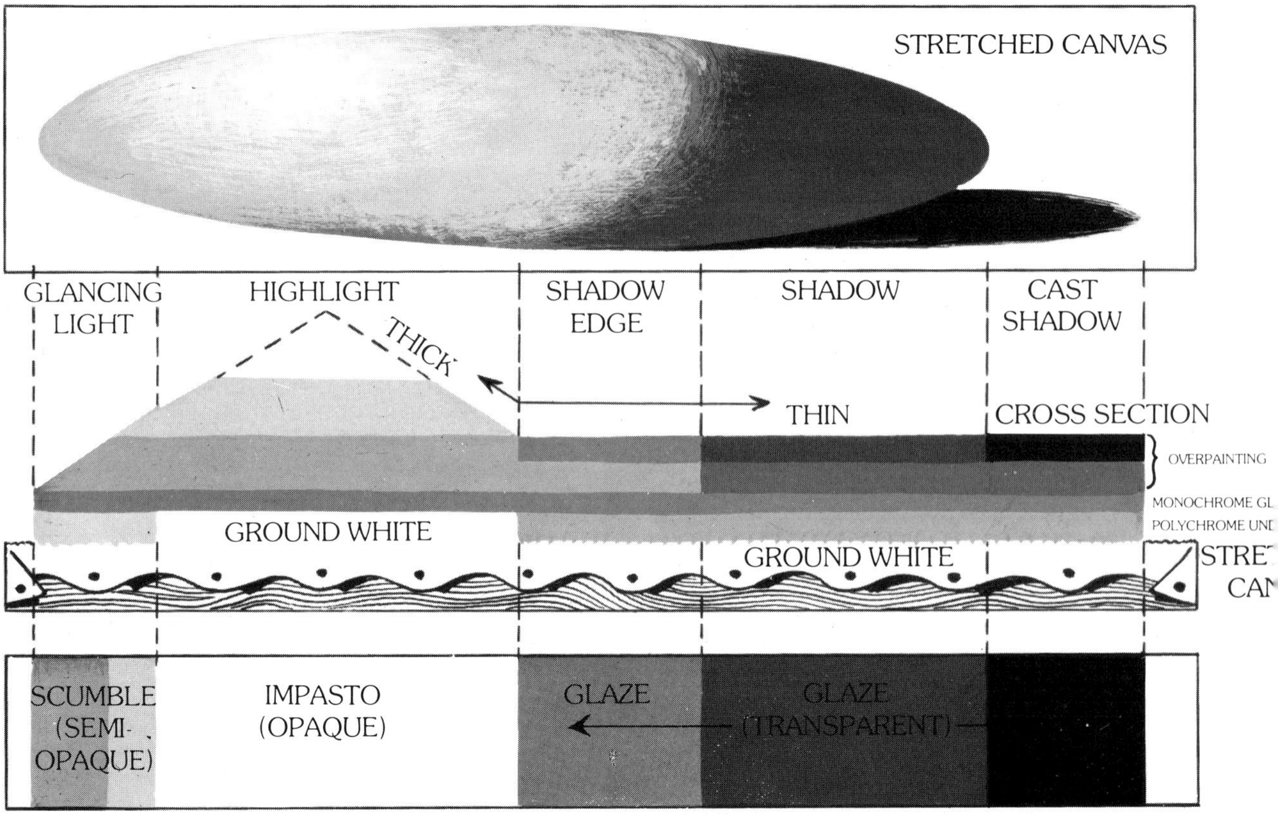

STRETCHED CANVAS

| GLANCING LIGHT | HIGHLIGHT | SHADOW EDGE | SHADOW | CAST SHADOW |

THICK ← → THIN CROSS SECTION

OVERPAINTING
MONOCHROME GL
POLYCHROME UN

GROUND WHITE GROUND WHITE

STRETCHED CANVAS

| SCUMBLE (SEMI-OPAQUE) | IMPASTO (OPAQUE) | GLAZE | ← GLAZE (TRANSPARENT) → | |

than did that of the light colors, would have permitted the white ground to "ghost" through. Thus the dark colors would lose their strength; the painting would weaken visibly. The light and dark pattern intended by the artist in the first place would be lost; shadows would no longer be shadows.

Another look at the van Eyck painting on page 27 reveals an unwanted double image of the man's right foot. Obviously, the foot had originally been positioned one way and then overpainted in another position. Undoubtedly, the original foot lay hidden until it was exposed when the painting was cleaned. Yet, such ghosting can occur when extremely thin dark glazes become too transparent with age.

In any event, following the customary medieval method, the Flemish painter then painted the usual egg tempera—or a variation of it—in every detail, as if it was to be the final job. At this point, the painting probably seemed typically airless, unnatural, and unearthly even though everything in the painting was recognizable; even though there were cast shadows. Light-keyed as the egg-water medium is, the Flemings must have pitched it even higher by keeping those areas meant to be richly dark in the final oil overpainting not much more than half dark or middle-toned in the egg tempera. Had they not done this, the final oil would not have appeared as brilliantly colored in the dark areas as it turned out to be.

The finished egg tempera was then allowed to dry for several weeks. Actually, an egg tempera is dry to the touch within seconds. Each stroke dries almost as it is being applied. However, the paint film is still a bit soft and the extra few weeks give the painting a chance to become firm and hard.

Directly over the dried and hardened egg tempera, the Flemish painters applied countless thin layers of oil paint varying in their transparency. What additives they used in their oil medium, a touch of varnish, perhaps beeswax, is unknown. Even the basic oil they used is unknown. It is possible that they concocted a very stable and workable oil emulsion, two or more oily binders like linseed oil and egg yolk, which are not soluble in each other, but which can be momentarily fused by the addition of powdered pigment, varnish, and a good shaking. The whole of this medium would have to be jolted frequently to keep the parts from separating into a suspension of individual layers. Whatever their medium,

Diagram of underpainting systems. Top: monochromatic (i.e., Titian). Bottom: polychromatic (i.e., Rubens).

the Flemish painters were able to change the surface appearance of painting masterfully. Van Eyck's *The Arnolfini Marriage* is an excellent example of the amazing "new look" that fairly burst upon the European art world during the fifteenth century. This new look—this painted illusion of natural light, solid form in space, depth, all smoothly rendered with remarkable contrasts of brilliant color—reflected the intense new human interest in the everyday world of the here and now. The artistic purpose of the Flemings, as it would soon be elsewhere, was frank realism. And the Flemings, with their oil glazing over water-based egg tempera, were the acknowledged masters of their age.

Several Florentine painters became interested in what the Flemish painters had accomplished and soon began some experiments in oil of their own. Among these artists were Domenico Veneziano (c. 1405-61); Andrea Del Castagno (c. 1421-57); and Alesso Baldovinetti (c. 1425-99). These three painters were the "moderns" of their day: restless, progressive thinkers who searched for new ways to express their ideas in paint.

Castagno made fresh contributions to the knowledge of anatomy and perspective. Veneziano tried to improve on the transparent oil tones, or *glazes*, painted over egg tempera, the method begun by the Flemings. He was able to achieve a softer effect and is known for his masterful sense of color. Baldovinetti experimented with the physics and chemistry of color and pigments while seeking new approaches to color harmonies. With all this activity, oil painting was slow in gaining the attention of other Florentine painters. The chief techniques were still the painting of egg-tempera panels and *frescoes,* wall paintings on wet or dry plaster.

None of these painters seemed yet to be as seriously involved with the new oil technique as their younger Venetian contemporary, Antonello da Messina (c.1430-79). Messina did considerable experimentation trying to improve on Veneziano's glazes. Using many of the van Eyck oil techniques and concentrating on detail in the Flemish manner, he was also able to achieve more naturalism in his work. Messina's *Portrait of a Man* on page 30 shows the same clarity and attention to detail as the van Eyck *Arnolfini Marriage.* And like van Eyck, Messina applied delicate thin transparent layers of oil paint over the egg tempera. Here and there Messina went back over the oil glazes with either egg tempera or an egg-oil emulsion to produce a more brilliant light. This is especially noticeable in the painting of the white shirt collar. Nevertheless, the expression on the man's face, particularly around his eyes, the overall warm tonality of the colors, the irregular tufts of hair on his forehead, the lack of symmetry or rhythmical spacing of the folds in his coat, the broad spread of light on his face, and the elimination of any harshness that could be caused by deep, sharp shadows, all contributed to the softer, more human appearance of the man.

However, all of these painters, Flemings and Italians alike, still used wood as the carrier, and gesso as the ground for their paintings, a combination of hard materials that helped to create the controlled clarity and minute detail that was so evident in much of their work. The fifteenth century, marked as it was by some of the greatest scientific investigations the world had known, was somewhat less certain artistically. Italian painters were in need of a new kind of painting surface, one that would remove the sharp, stiff look of medieval art that stubbornly hung on, reduce the sharpness of the individual parts of a painting, and allow the artist more flexibility in his treatment.

No one, as yet, had thought seriously of using lightweight, non-rigid material, such as paper or canvas, for painting major works of art. Canvas had been used chiefly for painted outdoor banners because it was light enough to be carried in parades and festivals. Paper, on the other hand, had been used a great deal for a highly specialized type of painting or brush drawing. More accurately, these renderings on paper were studies to explore the three-dimensional aspect of a particular object and were called *form* drawings. These papers were toned with a warm solution of gelatine and water to which had been added a small amount of color of the artist's own choosing—red, green, blue, rose, gray—any color that struck his fancy. Usually, the value of the color was about a middle tone or "halftone." On this toned paper the artist used a soft, fine brush to render the light areas of his work with a white pigment mixed with egg yolk and water; and the dark areas with black ink or a black pigment mixed with egg yolk and water. As in all techniques that use egg yolk as a binder, the color of the yolk has no effect whatever on the color of the pigment with which it is mixed. White remains white when mixed with egg yolk. At any rate, the artist never rendered a middle tone on his colored paper. Instead, he allowed the color of the paper to come between his lights and darks where it functioned as a middle tone.

As seen in illustration A at the top of page 5, the effect of such a

Over left: Detail of Venus and Adonis showing preliminary steps (as interpreted by the author). Over right: Detail of Venus and Adonis, by Peter Paul Rubens. Metropolitan Museum of Art, New York, N.Y.

brush drawing was one of sculpted relief—an effect that could not be achieved had the artist rendered the same object in blacks and grays on white paper as shown in illustration B below. Both illustrations are typical studies for the sleeve in the Titian portrait on the facing page, but the top illustration is a form drawing.

This frequent use of form drawing to study three dimensions was an obsession with late medieval and early Renaissance artists since exact knowledge of the solid form and structure of everything was basic to the creation of painted realities, an intense interest of these artists.

It was not until near the end of the fifteenth century that canvas for painting major works of art began to become popular. By that time, artists were more impressed by the effects of oil than they were by the effects of any water-based medium and had come to realize that the pliant, textured surface of canvas was more suitable to the more flexible oil medium than was rigid gessoed wood. And it did not take much experimentation for those artists of the Renaissance to find out that such a surface as canvas could give them the natural soft look they sought in their art rather than the unearthly hard look of a past era. Yet, it was not in Florence, where much of the Western world's artistic energies were anchored, that oil paint and canvas first flourished. It was in Venice where oil painting on canvas took root and grew to become the most widely used material for paintings.

The list of Venetian painters who used oil on canvas, as well as other media, is long. However, it remained for two of these painters, Titian and Giorgio da Castelfranco, known as Giorgione (c.1477-1510), to lay the foundation for the practice of oil painting on canvas that still survives. Giorgione, dead of the plague at thirty-three, did not live long enough to complete many paintings. Yet, he influenced a number of painters who followed him. Titian, on the other hand, lived to be an old man. His life spanned almost one third of the Italian Renaissance. Trained under Giovanni Bellini (c.1430-1516), Titian grew to be a superb craftsman who produced a rich, warm art of great lyric quality.

It was the system of underpainting that Titian used that determined his painting's final appearance. Basically, Titian's underpainting on linen canvas stretched taut over a wooden frame consisted of a highly opaque *priming* of white lead paint and a light-keyed, thinly applied, transparent wash called the *imprimatura*. Titian's imprimatura was usually reddish in color. Beneath the imprimatura was either a charcoal drawing or a painted outline of the general design. The transparent imprimatura blocked out the brightness of the white lead priming, but did not hide the charcoal drawing or painted outline. This wash consisted of either pigment mixed with a quick-drying oily resin—not to be confused with modern turpentinelike solvents—or glue size, gelatine dissolved in warm water to which was added a reddish pigment or a combination of reddish pigments.

When the imprimatura was thoroughly dry—overnight if the glue size was used, longer if an oily resin was used—a slightly deeper reddish oil color was painted in the dark areas only. Those areas meant to be light or lighter than a middle tone in the finished painting were painted pure white in the lightest areas and tints of white in the half-light areas. The white lead was permanent in color and durable as a paint film. It soaked up little oil or size leaving the surface fresh looking rather than spotty. It absorbed little light. Light rays passing through layers of applied transparent color would be bent, or refracted, by the white priming beneath. The light having passed into the painting through the transparent color would then be forced to pass outward again through the transparent color and so would add to the painting's brilliance. The whole of this preliminary work resulted in a one-color, or monochromatic, painting. The reddish tone of the underpainting would have a final effect on the overall warmness or warm tonality of the finished work, especially in the deep shadows.

Over this warmly colored monochromatic underpainting the overpainting was applied. As shown in diagram A on page 18, innumerable thin and transparent tints, or glazes, were painted in the shadow areas. Each glaze was darker than the one beneath. The shadow edges were *scumbled,* painted with opaque or partially opaque color to make the edges of the shadows softer and somewhat lighter. In the scumbles, each layer of paint was lighter in tone than the one beneath. Half-light areas, reflected lights—those lights on an object caused by light hitting a nearby surface rather than by a direct light hitting the object itself, and glancing lights—those lights that appear to catch light at an angle rather than head on were treated in the same way, by scumbling. *Highlights,* or those lights that are the brightest on a painted object, were applied *impasto*—with very opaque, *lean,* or less oily paint, thicker than the glazes and scumbles.

The glazes, scumbles, and impastos applied by Titian did not

Over left: Detail of possible ink underpainting for The Arnolfini Marriage, by Jan van Eyck (as interpreted by the author). Over right: The Arnolfini Marriage, by Jan van Eyck. National Gallery, London, England.

radically change the topography of the painting, its variable thickness and thinness, as much as that of some painters who came later: painters like Rembrandt Van Rijn (1606-69), the Dutch master. Rembrandt's impastos were extremely thick and noticeable; these can be clearly seen in his painting *Young Woman Bather* on page 35, especially in the painting of the highlights on the folds of the dress. Yet, Titian's surfaces, as thin as they seemed to be, were still more variable than the very smooth surfaces created by the Flemings who used mostly glazes in their oil over egg-tempera paintings. Also, because of the reddish underpainting, Titian's dark areas and shadows became warm and mellow while the light areas, which did not allow any reddish underpainting to come through, seemed cool and bright. Generally, backgrounds were completed first and foregrounds last along with whatever flesh tones had to be painted. Occasionally, the flesh tones were first glazed green or blue to increase the natural subsurface appearance of flesh colors. The very last thing to be painted were the highest lights and very deep accents. Often Titian, after not working on a painting for many months, made a number of changes in the overall effect and then applied a varnish to protect the painting's delicately glazed surface.

Interestingly enough, Titian's contemporary, Jacopo Robusti, known as Tintoretto (c. 1518-94), created a series of large paintings for Venice's Scuola di San Rocco which for four hundred years were thought to be oils. They were deep and full-bodied like oil paintings but much too blackish and low-keyed in their overall tonality—almost dirty looking. In fact, most experts thought that Tintoretto had used too much black paint. Eventually, during the early 1900's, these paintings were discovered to be size paintings—paintings executed with pigment bound by gelatine or a similar water-based glue and then varnished. They were not oil paintings. The varnish severely lowered the color values, giving the paintings an appearance similar to oil. In addition, an uncertain canvas priming beneath the color absorbed too much light adding a dark and somber look to what otherwise would have been a light-keyed painting. Another factor that contributed to the darkness of the paintings was that the color of the varnish deepened as time went by.

In its attempt to reverse the strength of the Protestant Reformation, the religious movement that was sweeping Europe and which, among other things, refused to recognize the power of the Catholic popes, the Catholic church began to encourage her painter employees to produce a style that would attract more attention. This was the painting style that came to be known as *baroque*—a light, elaborate, swirling, ornamental style. Actually, it was a change from the simple, straight and inactive appearance of things in painting, as seen in the work of Martini or van Eyck, to a heavier, more complicated, curved and active appearance as seen in the work of Peter Paul Rubens (1577-1640) of Flanders.

Catholic Flanders (now Belgium), a duchy of Spain, delighted in Rubens' lusty, swirling, complicated realism, as did the rest of Europe. Regardless of the subjects he painted—portraits, religious events, or mythological fantasies—his chief concern was making the objects in the paintings visually real, as if his subjects, however improbable and fanciful, were actually standing before our eyes. But to Rubens, a true-to-life portrayal was more than just painting something to look like what everyone expected it to look like. It meant giving a sense of the constant movement of real life to a nonmoving object, a painting. And it meant giving his painted figures a solid, moist, and fleshy appearance. For these reasons, many of Rubens' figures were painted unclothed, like the female and cupid figures in the detail from his *Venus and Adonis* on page 23. Nudity was a natural human state. And to Rubens, as well as other artists, this frank portrayal of the reality of the human form was the portrayal of the reality of life on this earth rather than an idea about some uncertain heaven or hell. Although Rubens was not the first artist, by any means, to paint nudes, he was among the first to paint them as if they looked like they could perspire. Without oil paint, the one medium that could produce variable, believable textures, the illusion of natural light and cast shadows, and nature's infinite colors, tones and depths, neither Rubens nor any other painter, whatever his personal style, could have created such an air of reality and a sense of being alive.

Born one year after the death of Titian, Rubens developed a variation of the Venetian master's system of underpainting, glazing, scumbling, and impasto. Instead of creating a one-color, or monochromatic, underpainting as shown in diagram A, at the top of page 18, Rubens first produced a multicolored, or *polychromatic,* underpainting —thin oil washes of middle to light tones that approximated the color of the final painting as shown in diagram B, at the bottom of page 18. The very bright lights that would finally appear in the finished painting were left the white of the ground or else repainted white. Over this polychrome imprimatura, Rubens painted a thin one-color glaze—usually gray, sometimes some other cool color. And it was over this monochrome glaze that the final overpainting was done. The diagram on page 22 shows the possible appearance of the Rubens process of underpainting. But instead of scumbling shadow edges as Titian had done before

him, he glazed these edges and created a more vibrant luminous look in his paintings. Also, as shown in diagram B, Rubens practically eliminated reflected light in some of his forms. This practice partially decreased the effects of light as seen in nature. Finally, Rubens altered his oil medium somewhat, thus giving his paintings a slicker, more slippery look overall, and a slightly thicker quality to the impasto. This alteration of the oil medium resulted from a greater use of a heavy oil called stand oil, made from boiled linseed oil. The stand oil was added to the paint in a partially diluted state. A certain amount of varnish was probably added to this mixture to harden it.

The Rubens workshop, staffed as it was by numerous workers, produced thousands of large oil paintings. And the Rubens system of painting developed into a highly methodical procedure that could be followed by the technicians and apprentices who worked on the paintings in order to keep all of the work similar in appearance—readily identified as a "Rubens."

The pleasant, courtly Rubens knowingly extended Titian's methods into new and more vigorous realms. His organized workshop, staffed by a score or more of technicians and apprentices, produced such artists as Anthony Van Dyck (1599-1641) who soon left Rubens' employ to work on his own. Van Dyck became a very successful portrait painter in England. There he established such a strong reputation that his work influenced the entire future of English portrait painting, which in turn influenced a later group of American portrait painters represented by such artists as John Singleton Copley (1738-1815).

Copley spent much of his working life in England. He left the American colonies as the American Revolution approached and spent some time traveling through Italy studying Italian painting before settling down in London. His portrait of *Mrs. Thomas Boylston,* an American, on page 32, shows the extent to which oil paint on canvas can be used to produce an almost unbelievable duplication of actual textures, in this case the magnificently painted satin dress. Here, the artist's purpose of painting something to look exactly as it was in real life was supported not only by the proper medium to achieve this natural effect but also by the painter's uncommon ability to use the oil medium effectively. And the vast knowledge and intense discipline necessary to manipulate the oil

Portrait of a Man, by Antonello da Messina. National Gallery, London, England.

medium to achieve purposeful realism was as evident in the paintings of John Singleton Copley as it was in the work of Peter Paul Rubens, however different their individual styles. This was despite the fact that Rubens died ninety-eight years before Copley was born and despite the fact that the seventeenth-century world of Rubens was much different from Copley's eighteenth century.

During the sixty-three years that Rubens lived, the know-how of the oil medium reached extraordinary levels of excellence. This wide knowledge, together with strenuous training, allowed most painters to bend this naturally flexible medium to their will. They began to invent individual oily-varnishy recipes to achieve whatever realistic effects they had in mind. Permanence was a secondary consideration. Stiff-haired "long" or "short rounds" had been brushes chiefly used. But now, flat, chisel-edge brushes, soft or stiff, were being introduced. These "flats" enabled painters to produce quick, clean, crisp slashes of color with less difficulty. They caused a radical change in the surface appearance of paintings such as the late work of Rembrandt and Frans Hals (1580-1666), another Dutch painter. Also, by this time, slow-drying oil paint, which had been prepared in small quantities as needed, was ground in such quantity that it could be stored in sheep's bladders for continuous use—something that could not be done with egg-yolk-tempered pigment, for instance. The egg would often rot and produce an unbearable odor. In addition, it was extremely difficult to prepare large quantities of egg-tempered paint.

Hals's portrait *A Naval Officer,* on page 36, is an example of a direct approach called *alla prima* painting. It had little to do with glazes and scumbles—only with thick, "juicy" paint. There is a marked difference in the loose, casual way Hals painted the officer's sleeve and the less casual way Titian treated the sleeve in his portrait on page 4 and in the precise, smooth manner van Eyck handled the folds of the clothing in his *Arnolfini Marriage.* Yet, these three painters, all of whom approached the portrayal of reality differently, nevertheless succeeded, each in his own way, to convey a unique sense of reality. Each of them made the viewer of their paintings believe that what he was looking at was indeed lifelike.

Alla prima painting, as practiced by Frans Hals, was a forerunner of twentieth-century paint handling. This method of rapidly applying

Mrs. Thomas Boylston, by John Singleton Copley. Fogg Art Museum, Boston, Mass.

thick paint to a constantly wet surface seemed to suit Hals's personality with his *joie de vivre* and lack of patience in executing the various stages of a multilayered painting. Although Hals's paintings were done more quickly than those of the other masters, it must not be assumed that he merely splashed one layer of paint on his canvas without any preparation. While the total effect is one of complete spontaneity, Hals's canvases were usually prepared with a gray ground and a somewhat sketchy drawing. These paintings were often completed in one sitting.

Rembrandt, on the other hand, a meticulous craftsman, used the Titian-Rubens system of glazes, scumbles, and impastos to suit himself. But he turned away from an overall brightness to create large, deep, luminous shadows of thin paint that set off smaller light areas painted with dramatic bursts of brilliant heavy paint, a technique clearly seen in his *Young Woman Bather* on page 35. All of this was varnished and revarnished over the years, giving the paintings a brownish-yellow appearance which deepened the shadows further and cut down on some of the brilliant lights. This amberish effect, often called the golden glow, is an effect that Rembrandt himself might have marveled at, but an effect which was not present in a newly finished work. The startling drama of Rembrandt's painting comes vividly alive when the thick, dirty, brownish-yellow aging layers of varnish are removed and the cleaned painting is returned to the crisp appearance and vivid contrasts that Rembrandt himself intended and saw. Rembrandt's powerful contrasts of light and dark were not unlike the work of the Italian illusionist Caravaggio who died when Rembrandt was about three years old. Caravaggio's paint handling, however, as seen in his *Crucifixion of Saint Peter* on page 9, was more even, thinner, and far less atmospheric, despite its striking photographic quality.

Elsewhere, the Dutch were creating carefully rendered *genre* paintings—scenes of everyday life. These were bought for the homes of the newly rich Dutch middle class. Casual scenes like *A Dutch Courtyard* by Pieter de Hooch (1629-c. 1684) on page 45 were not casually painted, nor did painters like de Hooch interpret nature casually. These painters, Gerard Ter Borch (1611-81), Gerrard Dou (1613-75), Gabriel Metsu (1630-67), Jan Vermeer (1632-75)—known as the *Little Dutchmen*—painted nature as nature is visually. They could not have achieved their effects without sound knowledge of drawing, perspective, anatomy, and the structure and texture of all solid objects as they appear in different

Young Woman Bather, by Rembrandt. National Gallery, London, England.

spaces and under variable light. Nor could they have done this without oil paint. The Little Dutchmen were not uncertain craftsmen. They painted systematically: underpainting to overpainting; background to foreground; middle tones roughed in lean; transparent glazes next; light areas brought up, opaque and impasto; more dark glazes; more middle-tone scumbling; lights and darks constantly adjusted; the focus sharpened; finally, highlights here, deep accents there, and the work was done. Hindered by the slow drying of the paint, an artist usually worked on several paintings at the same time.

This orderly bringing to life of a painting was the general European practice. It was about the same for German, English, French, or Spanish painters as it was for the Italian, Flemish, and Dutch, regardless of their different ideas about nature, realism, and style. And the whole process of oil painting, from start to finish, was chiefly established in fifteenth-century Flanders and sixteenth-century Italy. Even the Greek painter who studied in Italy and settled in Spain, Domenico Theotocopuli (c. 1541-1614), better known as El Greco, relied on step by step method to achieve the loose movement and shimmering color that set such paintings as his *Saint Martin and The Beggar* (page 46) apart from everyone else's.

El Greco's purpose and interest in realism was aimed not so much at the actual appearance of objects as they seemed to the eye, but at the changing appearance of objects as he thought and felt about them. This was an inward reality, a reality of the mind, rather than an outward reality, a reality of the eye. The remarkable aspect of El Greco's work was his use of leaping, shivering lights and elongated, almost rubbery, figures to create in his art the seeming throb of life. Like Rubens, who came later, and whose style was different, El Greco's painting was concerned with the living, moving force within objects and people, not merely their outward appearance.

Another Spaniard, Diego Velazquez (1599-1660), purposefully painted his backgrounds thin and hazy with only a suggestion of detail. The foregrounds were always sharper. As seen in the detail of his oil painting *The Surrender of Breda*, frontispiece of this book, Velazquez created three distinct areas of distance called *picture planes*. The first of

Portrait of a Naval Officer, by Frans Hals. National Gallery, Washington, D.C. Over left: Monsieur Rivière, by Jean Auguste Dominique Ingres. The Louvre, Paris, France. Over right: The Grand Canal, Venice, by Edouard Manet. Provident Securities Co., San Francisco, Calif.

these, and the picture plane closest to the viewer, was the foreground. Here Velazquez painted large groups of figures in some detail in warm tones of vivid lights and darks. With less contrast and cooler colors, he painted the middle ground or that distance between the background, the picture plane that represents the farthest distance, and the foreground. The background was painted with little contrast, no sharp detail, and in the coolest blues and greens.

In this way, Velazquez gave an impression of airy distance—an effect called atmospheric or aerial perspective. As Hals, Rubens, Rembrandt, and El Greco were all forerunners of twentieth-century personally expressive painting, or *expressionism,* Velazquez signaled the approach of modern *impressionism,* the painting of objects as they are seen and altered by changing light at varying distances either at a momentary glance or over a longer period of time; the impressionist idea that grew slowly, unevenly from seventeenth-century Spain until it came to its full development among a number of "radical" painters of nineteenth-century France.

From the seventeenth century to the nineteenth century the painting styles changed frequently as did the style of life and politics. But it was mostly style that was changing in painting rather than the discovery of new methods of applying paint. The medium, too, remained unchanged; it was still oil. Not even the English artists who began to introduce transparent watercolor during the eighteenth century could replace oil painting in the same way that oil painting replaced egg-tempera painting and fresco during the fifteenth and sixteenth centuries.

The baroque quietly slid into the *rococo,* a more gracefully active style, light and fragile. The rococo slipped into the *neoclassic* style, a rebirth of what some artists thought was the image of ancient Greece and perhaps Rome. There were groups of artists who thought that the ideas of other artists in the past were more important than their own "new" ideas and often mixed elements that did not blend well. These were the *eclectics.* Others turned away from everyday surroundings and invented imaginary scenes. Some of these artists were called *romantics.* But whatever style or idea the oil painter pursued he still aimed for realism—or at least that unexplainable illusion in a painting that could convince a viewer that what he was looking at was true to life. Whoever the artist, and whatever the idea, the general application of oil to canvas remained unchanged, for the most part. If there was any change at all, it was the slow drifting away from the careful preparation of the carrier. Painters were becoming interested in quick results and Titian or Rubens-like underpainting was too complicated and time-consuming. Besides, men like Titian and Rubens had a variety of workers, apprentices, students, and technicians to do such things as underpainting and numerous other tedious jobs. By the beginning of the eighteenth century, most painters were working alone or with few assistants.

Among the French, Jean Fragonard (1732-1806) painted delicate scenes of life and love for the royalty before the French Revolution. After the Revolution and with the rise to power of Napoleon, France dreamed of empire and so did some of her artists. They were the neoclassicists: Jacques Louis David (1748-1825); François Gérard (1770-1837); and Jean Auguste Dominique Ingres (1780-1867). These painters, especially David and Ingres, typified the spirit of the "classic revival" in France. The quality of their *draftsmanship* or drawing skill was remarkably proficient. In fact, Ingres insisted that the pictorial structure, or basic drawing, of a painting was more important than its color. Nevertheless, using a varnishy oil medium and a planned step by step method, Ingres created such smooth and brilliant canvases that most untrained people who look at them are unaware of any painted surface—only the photographic reality of the subject. Ingres' masterfully controlled, sharply focused photographic-like portraits, *Monsieur Rivière,* for example, on page 38, did exactly what he meant them to do—created a perfect picture excluding the flaws inherent in nature.

But some Frenchmen were weary of Ingres' "impersonal" naturalism and the strict discipline he and others demanded. Painters like Théodore Géricault (1791-1824) and Eugène Delacroix (1798-1863) grumbled that realism should be less perfectly created because things in nature were simply not as perfect as Ingres painted them. They argued that color was more important than draftsmanship. And they insisted that painters like Ingres, who adhered to a set of rigid rules for the painting of realism, were actually out of touch with reality. They were academicians, much too interested in their rules of perspective, flesh painting, composition and the like.

Soon, however, a new machine would be invented for picture making that would produce a picture of exactly what its "eye" or lens saw—a camera. Louis Jacques Daguerre (1787-1851), a French painter, perfected a type of photograph during the 1830's that was used chiefly for portraits. The process, at first, was known as daguerreotype. Later it was refined and called photography. This mechanical means for imitating the appearance of nature set in motion an argument that continued among artists and non-artists alike for the next hundred years or

more. It was a clear challenge to the purpose of painters; whether they should continue to produce lifelike pictures through representational art now that the camera had been invented; and a challenge to the merits of oil painting to achieve this realism now that a film could do the same.

The gradual change that overtook French painting, if not most of the painting of western Europe during the early 1800's, was not a radical change in methods of applying paint. The change that began to take place in the appearance of paintings was philosophical—a growing, questioning attitude regarding the nature of reality; how we see and feel about what we see; and the usefulness of oil paint in creating absolute illusions of "natural" appearances. Much of this rethinking was brought about by the Industrial Revolution and the increasing mechanization of Western society. Once again, as in the late medieval period, man had begun to reconsider his ideas about the world he lived in—not from the "hereafter" to the "now," but from an age-old agricultural way of life to a new industrial way of life. And this rethinking would continue into the twentieth century. There is little doubt, too, that the invention of photography in the early 1800's, a mechanical device for picture making, began to play a major role in deepening the confusion among painters and art patrons everywhere as to the nature of realism, naturalism, representational, or true-to-life painting. Nevertheless, unlike the shift in attitude from the Middle Ages to the Renaissance which produced a definite change in painting medium and method to alter the look of art, there was no clear-cut switch during the 1800's. If there was any change in oil painting method, it was the more widespread use of faster, direct, alla prima painting, with little or no underpainting. Moreover, there seemed to be less concern for sharply rendered detail and more "jumping around" the canvas with all parts of the painting being worked on at the same time. The construction of paintings was becoming looser and freer.

The French artist Edouard Manet (1832–83) reflected this shifting attitude about painted realities more than anyone else at the time. There was an echo of medieval flat tone in his early work, although the basic drawing in the painting was more dimensional. There was a hint of the sketchy atmospheric quality of Velazquez whom he much admired. In his later career, Manet's paintings became more involved with the

A Sunday Afternoon at the Grande Jatte, by George Seurat. Chicago Art Institute, Chicago, Ill.

nature of light and swiftly caught impressions. With such canvases as *The Grand Canal, Venice,* reproduced on page 39, Manet drew further away from the realist tradition represented by his countryman Ingres, and began to support a new idea called *pleinairism,* which was the painting of natural daylight by breaking up the color on the canvas almost as if one were viewing it through a glass prism. Actually, what Manet created in *The Grand Canal, Venice* was a well-thought-out patchwork of loosely applied color over a white primed canvas that had little or no underpainting. Except for the dark accents provided by the gondolas, the painting is essentially high keyed. Both the dark accents and middle tones—the blues of the poles, for instance—are thickly painted. The bright whites on the poles are also impasto, or heavily painted. All of those light tones between the middle tones and the bright whites, such as those of the building or sky, are thin and somewhat transparent, permitting the white ground underneath to have its brightening effect. The result is a canvas that fairly sparkles with daylight. And from a short distance, the loosely painted scene, with sketchy detail, seems to glitter from both the warm sunlight and the cool reflected light of the water. But unlike the earlier El Greco whose shimmering color grew out of an inward reality, Manet's shimmering color had the purpose of duplicating an outward reality—the appearance of natural light.

Manet's interest in pleinairism coincided with the work of Claude Monet (1840-1926), Camille Pissarro (1830-1903), and Auguste Renoir (1841-1919), who were searching for a new approach to realism, the realism of painted daylight in a fleeting moment of time and distance called impressionism. These painters did not sit in their studios and decide what daylight looked like. They took their paints and canvases outdoors and painted the ever-changing variations of natural light as it flooded their surroundings.

The attempt of the impressionists to paint the appearance of daylight was, in a sense, a scientific investigation. It was not much different from the mathematical studies of linear perspective made by medieval painters.

One by-product of pleinairism and impressionism was a very precise application of color by another Frenchman, Georges Seurat (1859-91). This was called *pointillism,* a method in which small dabs of pure color are applied side by side so that they appear to blend at a distance.

A Dutch Courtyard, by Pieter de Hooch. National Gallery, Washington, D.C.

Seurat did not originate the method of applying color in small dabs. This had been done before by earlier artists. Jacques Louis David occasionally dabbed paint on a canvas. However, it is doubtful that these earlier painters were concerned with the same final optical effects that later interested Seurat. More than likely their dabbing was a preliminary step to give a slight tooth to a very smoothly primed canvas in order to provide a surface better able to grip the many layers of paint that would follow.

This preliminary step of dabbing spots of oil color to keep the final overpainting from slipping on very slick surfaces is still used today. One such technique involves the application of oil paint to a water-based gesso ground—the same gesso used as a ground for egg-tempera painting. In this method a hard untextured panel such as wood or masonite is coated with about four or five layers of the gesso. Sometimes a black ink underpainting is executed on the gesso, sometimes not. The gesso itself is much too absorbent to receive oil paint directly, unless the artist who oil paints on such a surface wants a flat, chalky, dull effect. To retain brilliance of color and dramatic tonal values, the water-based gesso would have to be treated to make it nonabsorbent. This is quickly done by applying several coats of a very thin mixture of clear shellac and alcohol. The shellacked gesso now becomes the surface upon which the artist will apply his color. However, this new surface is so glassy and slick that it is extremely difficult to keep the color from sliding all over it making the painting hard to control. To prevent this and to give the surface a better tooth, the artist must dab his color as a preliminary step. When these painstaking dabs dry, the artist then proceeds to brush his final colors in any way he wishes. One of the startling effects of a painting executed in this manner is the brilliant, luminous clarity recalling similar qualities in the oils of the early Flemings.

Color, as the impressionists very well knew, was a complicated matter. All colors have certain physical and chemical properties that give them their individual appearances. Individual colors each have changing aspects under different lights. Most colors can be made to change their appearance by surrounding them with other colors. A bright yellow surrounded by black will seem more intense than that same yellow surrounded by a dazzling white. The painter, as an artist, must deal with all of these myriad problems regarding his application of

Saint Martin and The Beggar, by El Greco. National Gallery, Washington, D.C.

color, his choice of colors, their combinations, and his own personal preferences. The pointillist Georges Seurat, in his painting *A Sunday Afternoon at the Grande Jatte*, a detail of which is shown on page 42, tried to capture the sparkling luminosity of light by mixing colors in a very purposeful way. Instead of mixing blue and red together into one violet color, he painted a blue dab next to a red dab and let them seem to melt together into a violet when seen from a distance. Green was made the same way—a dab of blue next to a dab of yellow. At no time did Seurat underpaint the darks or any other part of the painting. He allowed the pure white ground of the canvas to increase the brilliance of all the colors. For the most part, he simply kept the darks or shadow areas cooler than the light areas.

Whether or not Seurat's *Sunday Afternoon at the Grand Jatte* appears to have the same natural appearance as Ingres' *Monsieur Rivière*, or Caravaggio's *Crucifixion of Saint Peter*, or Copley's portrait *Mrs. Thomas Boylston*, is a matter for endless discussion. Yet, one thing is certain: Seurat was reaching for the very same natural effect seen in the actual world that had interested oil painters since the fifteenth-century Flemings startled the Italians with their ideas about "realism" and their new oil medium.

The French impressionists, Seurat included, made a profound technical contribution to the use of oil paint to visually express an illusion of the world we live in. Now, about a hundred years later, French impressionism still stands as perhaps the most influential modern alteration of oil paint application to capture external realities—how we see what we see rather than what we feel about what we see.

Throughout the history of all painting there have been nearly as many recipes and strange ingredients as there have been painters and paintings. Some of these strange concoctions were so unsatisfactory that paintings fell apart soon after they were completed. Some had to be continuously restored to their original appearance. Many painters considered their oil medium recipes so important to their artistic and business success that they were kept secret.

Today, there are as many varied ways of applying paint as there are exotic paint media, ideas about method, and places to see paintings. The most important variation that changed the surface appearance of oil paintings during our twentieth century and influenced the look of much of the painting of our time was the use of a trowel-like tool called a painting knife. Just before the turn of the century some artists put aside their brushes and began to apply their color with the stiff palette knives used to scrape a *palette* clean or scrape unwanted paint from a canvas. This was a speedy method for spreading color shapes on the canvas with some thickness to create planes, spaces, and textures. It was alla prima painting with a slightly different twist. But more than that it was a direct outgrowth of the pleinairist-impressionist system of breaking up the color on the canvas. Soon, very flexible painting knives were developed with various-shaped blades that made it easier for the more modern artists to control and refine this method of application.

The use of the painting knife seemed to come at a time when many artists began to think that painting need not necessarily represent the external appearance of nature. Still applying oils in the usual methods, twentieth-century artists gradually began to create new, bold images that had little or nothing to do with the accurate representation of nature. From the first decade of the twentieth century to the present time painters became more and more preoccupied with the personality of whatever it was they painted rather than with the actual look of it. They distorted nature to communicate what they felt about what they painted. They tried to reach the essence—the inner spirit—of something, some idea. They delighted in color for its own sake, in shapes and forms and textures that were totally imaginative and had no real counterpart in the natural environment.

As the twentieth-century artist moved in the direction of a more personal expressive art, his work became more inventive. What he painted could not be seen anywhere except in the painting. Yet, while he changed his images, he did not appreciably alter the old proven methods of applying oil paint.

By the middle of the twentieth century, painters had liberated themselves from every acceptable tradition about what paintings were supposed to look like and embarked on a whole new approach with regard to the purpose of painting—nonrepresentational. As a result, oil paint, which had originally come into use to recreate nature, no longer seemed to require complicated processes, exacting and careful craftsmanship. There were new purposes now and these purposes had nothing to do with real life painted illusions. Oil had run its course for most of those artists who had turned away from representational art. New and different media were in the offing and contemporary artists began to seriously explore and experiment with more modern technology, one that would better suit the ideas of the twentieth century.

For the painter, the heart of the matter is to put idea, medium, and method of application together in such a way that his creative purpose is served and understood, and his work is reasonably durable. The trick is to know when all these things are in harmony and working well. Anyone who paints or wants to paint should know how differently various media behave. And anyone interested in creating illusions of reality should compare the effects of different paint media.

If, for example, one were to paint a grassy field against a cloudy sky in schoolroom poster paint, transparent watercolor, an opaque watercolor called gouache, egg tempera, or casein, oil, and the more modern acrylics, the differences would be immediately apparent. Depending on the purpose for which each of these paintings was used, each would have its own flavor. However, although the scene would be recognizable in each of the paintings, its textures, atmosphere, light, shadow, form, color, tones, and distances would vary greatly with the medium. Moreover, the scene painted with oil would appear to be the least artificial of all. Oil paint remains the one medium above all others that can best reproduce atmospheric realism and the total almost absolute illusion of the world we live in.

For the past one hundred and fifty years, man has been changing his ideas about nature, realities, the world he lives in, and even the worlds beyond—the worlds of space and life elsewhere in the universe. Man's knowledge, ideas, and visions about himself in relation to all this vastness are expanding so rapidly that at times he is confused by them. Nevertheless, someday, the man of the future, like those who came before—medieval man or Renaissance man—will come to some definite conclusions about his new self. When he does, he will bring to these new visions—to his new understanding of life, here and beyond—a new and suitable painting medium to express it all. It is already happening.

GLOSSARY

Alla prima — Direct applications of paint without complicated underpainting, scumbles, or glazes. Usually, the painting is worked on and completed in a constantly wet state.

Atmospheric Perspective — The illusion of distance on a flat surface by means of softening or blurring those forms or cooling those colors in a bluish haze that are not in the foreground. Sometimes called *aerial perspective*.

Baroque — A very ornamental, swirling style of painting that was initiated during the late sixteenth century. Characteristic are its sense of motion and grandeur. Often baroque artists attempted to join architecture, sculpture, and painting into an entity.

Binder — Any substance used to hold together pigment particles or to cause pigment to adhere to the surface to which it has been applied.

Carrier — Any untreated surface, such as wood or canvas, upon which a painting is created after the surface is treated.

Descriptive Line — A line drawn to indicate the shape or form of an object.

Draftsmanship — Drawing skill.

Eclectics — Artists who chose to incorporate elements or philosophical ideas from many eras in their paintings.

Egg Tempera — Pigment ground in water and mixed with egg yolk.

Expressionism — Art in which the artist is more concerned with expressing his emotional reaction to an object or situation rather than approaching his subject on a naturalistic basis. Very prevalent in German art of the twentieth century.

Form — A shape having three dimensions: height, width, and depth.

Fresco — A water-based painting executed either on wet or dry plaster walls.

Genre — A painting of the daily activity of ordinary people.

Gesso — A white substance made of whiting (i.e., refined chalk derived from calcium carbonate), gelatine, and water, applied to a carrier as a warm liquid and used as a painting ground when dry and hard.

Glazes — Thin transparent layers of color, applied over layers of

	solid color, each successive layer darker than the one beneath.
Ground	The prepared surface for painting. It is usually white in color.
Highlight	The lightest light in a painting, which seems to emanate from a natural (i.e., sunlight), artificial (i.e., electric-light bulb), or imaginary light source within the painting.
Illusionist	An artist whose purpose is to duplicate the actual appearance of nature.
Impasto	Heavy "pasty" layers of paint usually applied to the brightest areas of an oil painting.
Impressionism	A late-nineteenth-century artistic movement concerned with the effects of natural daylight upon objects, figures, scenes, and the like, caught in a momentary, almost casual glance. Impressionism began among French artists as a technical investigation of the painting of daylight to create more natural and less artificial images.
Imprimatura	A transparent color wash brushed onto the white ground before an underpainting is begun.
Intensity	The strength or weakness of a color—its brightness or dullness.
Key	The overall brightness or darkness of a painting.
Lean	Paint applied with as little of the vehicle as possible—for example, containing little oil.
Line	A narrow stroke which varies in length and width but which has no measurable edge, depth, or third dimension.
Linear Perspective	The illusion of distance or depth on a flat surface by means of lines converging on a horizon point or on other selected visual points, causing objects to appear smaller as they recede into the picture planes.
Medium	The substance or liquid into which pigments are ground to make them usable as paint, such as oil, size, egg yolk, and gum arabic.
Monochrome	A one-color painting.
Neoclassicism	The eighteenth-century revival of artistic styles of ancient Greece and Rome.
Opaque Color	A dense paint that does not permit light to pass through it, thus completely hiding or covering whatever is beneath. Nontransparent.

Overpainting	The final application of glazes, scumbles, and impastos in oil painting. The application of any paint over an underpainting or imprimatura.
Palette	Usually a flat board or tray upon which the painter mixes his oil colors.
Picture Planes	Imaginary flat vertical areas which indicate zones of distance within a painting. The three chief planes of a painting are the *foreground*, the area of the painting represented to be nearest the viewer; the *background*, the area of the painting represented to be farthest from the viewer; and the *middle ground*, the area equidistant between the foreground and the background.
Pigment	Coloring matter—paint.
Pleinairism	A nineteenth-century French technique of creating the illusion of daylight by breaking up the color into irregularly shaped patches as if viewing the light through a glass prism. Pleinairism was the forerunner of French impressionism and the technique called *pointillism*.
Pointillism	A late-nineteenth-century French method of painting, in which small dabs of color are applied to the ground, side by side, so that they appear to blend smoothly at a distance. The intention of the artists was to arrive at more vivid coloring by means of this technique rather than by mixing the colors on the palette.
Polychrome	A painting executed in more than one color.
Priming	Preparing the carrier with glue size or other materials in order to apply the ground upon which the actual painting is rendered.
Rendering	The particular graphic treatment of a subject such as a "line" rendering or a "tone" rendering. Also, the manner of applying pigment to a surface.
Rococo	An eighteenth-century style of very delicately curved ornamental shapes and forms that followed the baroque style but which was lighter in feeling and less grandiose.
Romanticism	A nineteenth-century painting style that concentrated on subjects not directly connected with the obvious, current realities of life. The atmosphere of the paintings took on greater significance than the naturalistic objects themselves.
Scumble	Thin opaque or semiopaque layers of color with each

	successive layer lighter than the one beneath showing some of the color of the previous layers.
Size	A glue substance—usually gelatine and water—used for priming, preparation of gesso, a painting medium, and a variety of other applications.
Structural Line	A line drawn to indicate the shape or form of an object and the relationship or arrangement of all its parts.
Tapestry	A large heavy ornamentally woven fabric used, primarily, as a wall hanging.
Tonality	The lightness or darkness of a painting. Also, the coolness or warmness of a painting.
Tone	The lightness or darkness of a color. Also, the coolness or warmness of a color.
Underpainting	A preliminary painting—usually in one color—applied as a beginning step in some painting techniques.
Values	The degrees of difference between the lightest and darkest tones of a color.
Vehicle	The substance or liquid mixed with previously ground pigments to make them more workable.

INDEX

Acrylics, 50
Alla prima painting, 33, 49
Arnolfini Marriage, The (Jan van Eyck), 20, 25, 33
Atmospheric perspective, 13, 40

Baldovinetti, Alesso, 20
Baroque style, 28-29, 40
Beggar, The (El Greco), 37, 47
Bellini, Giovanni, 24
Binder, 6, 16
    defined, 3
Brush, flat, 33

Camera, invention of, 41
Canvas, use of, 21, 24
Caravaggio, Michelangelo Merisi da, 34
    Crucifixion of Saint Peter by, 8, 14, 34, 48
Carrier, wood as, 16, 21
Casein, 6, 50
Castagno, Andrea Del, 20
Catholic popes, 11-12, 15, 28
Cennini, Cennino d'Andrea, 2
Charcoal drawing, 17, 24, 25
China, ancient, 3
Colors, 47-48
    intensity of, in oil painting, 14
    physical and chemical properties of, 20, 47
Copley, John Singleton, 31, 33
    Mrs. Thomas Boylston by, 31, 48
Crucifixion of Saint Peter, The (Caravaggio), 8, 14, 34, 48

Daguerre, Louis Jacques, 41
Daguerreotype, 41
David, Jacques Louis, 41, 47
Delacroix, Eugène, 41
Descriptive line, 8
Dou, Gerrard, 34
Draftsmanship, 41
Dutch Courtyard, A (de Hooch), 34, 44
Dutchmen, Little, 34, 37

Eclecticism, 40
Egg tempera, 6, 8, 10, 15, 16, 19, 20, 28, 47, 50
Egg yolk, as binder, 6, 8, 16, 19, 21
Expressionism, 40

Flemish painters, fifteenth-century, 14, 15-20, 21, 37, 47, 48

Florentine painters, 16, 20
Form drawing, 21, 24
Fragonard, Jean, 41
France, nineteenth-century, 2, 41, 43
Fresco, 20

Gérard, François, 41
Géricault, Théodore, 41
Gesso, 16, 17, 21, 47
Giorgione, 24
Glaze, 25, 29, 31, 34
    over egg tempera, 20, 28
Glue size, 16, 17, 25
Golden-glow effect, 34
Gouache, 50
Grand Canal, Venice, The (Manet), 37, 44
Greco, El, 37, 40, 44
    Beggar by, 37, 47
    Saint Martin by, 37, 47
Greece, ancient, 3, 40
Ground, gesso, 17, 19, 21, 47

Hals, Frans, 33, 34, 40
    Naval Officer by, 33, 37
Highlights, applied impasto, 25
Hooch, Pieter de, *Dutch Courtyard* by, 34, 44
Humanism, 12

Illuminations, manuscript, 14
Impasto, 25, 28, 29, 31, 34, 44
Impressionism, 40, 44, 47, 48, 49
Imprimatura, 24, 25, 29
Industrial Revolution, 43
Ingres, Jean Auguste Dominique, 8, 41, 44
    Monsieur Rivière by, 37, 41, 48
Intensity, color, in oil painting, 14
Italy
    art guilds of, 15
    sixteenth-century, 2

Knife, palette, 48-49

Lean paint, 25
Libro dell'Arte, Il (Cennini), 2
Line
    descriptive, 8
    as two-dimensional stroke, 8
Linear perspective, 13, 44
Little Dutchmen, 34, 37

Locking agent, *see* Binder

Manet, Edouard, 43-44
    Grand Canal of Venice by, 37, 44
Manuscript illuminations, 14
Martini, Simone, 29
    Saint John the Evangelist by, 6, 8, 10
Medium, defined, 3
Memling, Hans, 14
Messina, Antonello da, 20
    Portrait of a Man by, 20, 31
Metsu, Gabriel, 34
Middle Ages, 14, 43
Monet, Claude, 2, 44
Monochromatic painting, 17, 19, 25
Monsieur Rivière (Ingres), 37, 41, 48
Mrs. Thomas Boylston (Copley), 31, 48

Naturalism, 41, 43
Naval Officer, A (Hals), 33, 37
Neoclassic style, 40, 41
Nudes, painting of, 29

Oil painting, 3, 6, 8, 12, 13, 14, 37, 49, 50
    color intensity in, 14
    Flemish, fifteenth-century, 14, 15-20, 21, 37, 47, 48
    slow drying time of, 14, 33
    and water media, differences between, 8, 10, 11, 14
    See also Painting
Opaque color, 17, 25
Overpainting, 17, 25, 47

Painting
    alla prima, 33, 49
    baroque, 28-29, 40
    and Eastern character, 12
    expressionist, 40
    Flemish, 14, 15-20, 21, 37, 47, 48
    Florentine, 16, 20
    impressionist, 40, 44, 47, 48, 49
    keys of, 6, 11
    monochromatic, 17, 19, 25
    neoclassic, 40, 41
    nonrepresentational, 49
    of nudes, 29
    oil, *see* Oil painting
    polychromatic, 19, 29
    representational, 43
    rococo, 40
    water-based, *see* Water-based painting
    and Western character, 12
Painting knife, 48-49
Palette, 49
Paper, for brush drawing, 21

Perspective
    atmospheric, 13, 40
    linear, 13, 44
Photography, 41, 43
Picture planes, 37, 40
Pigment, defined, 3
Pissarro, Camille, 44
Pleinairism, 44, 49
Pointillism, 44, 48
Polychromatic painting, 19, 29
Popes, Catholic, 11-12, 15, 28
Portrait of a Man (Messina), 20, 31
Portrait of a Man (Titian), 3, 10
Portrait of a Naval Officer (Hals), 33, 37
Portrait painting, 31
Priming, white lead, 24
Protestant Reformation, 15, 28

Realism, 16, 29, 33, 37, 41, 43, 44, 48, 50
Reformation, Protestant, 15, 28
Rembrandt Van Rijn, 28, 33, 34, 40
    Young Woman Bather by, 28, 34
Renaissance, 12, 16, 24, 43
Renoir, Auguste, 44
Resin, oily, use of, 25
Rococo style, 40
Roman Catholic popes, 11-12, 15, 28
Romanticism, 40
Rome, ancient, 3, 11, 40
Rubens, Peter Paul, 19, 29, 31, 33, 37, 40, 41
    Venus and Adonis by, 21, 29
    workshop of, 31

Saint John the Evangelist (Martini), 6, 8, 10
Saint Martin (El Greco), 37, 47
Scumbling, 25, 29, 34
Seurat, Georges, 44, 47, 48
    Sunday Afternoon at the Grande Jatte by, 43, 48
Shellac, for gesso, 47
Stand oil, 31
Structural line, 8
Sunday Afternoon at the Grande Jatte, A (Seurat), 43, 48
Surrender of Breda, The (Velazquez), 37

Tapestry, 16
Ter Borch, Gerard, 34
Tintoretto, 28
Titian, 19, 24, 25, 28, 29, 31, 33, 40, 41
    Portrait of a Man by, 3, 10
Tonality, 6, 21

Underpainting, 17, 24, 29, 41, 47
Untempered paint, 3

Values, 8
Van Der Goes, Hugo, 14
Van Der Weyden, Roger, 14
Van Dyck, Anthony, 31
Van Eyck, Hubert, 14, 15
Van Eyck, Jan, 14, 15, 20, 29
    Arnolfini Marriage by, 20, 25, 33
Vehicle, defined, 3
Velazquez, Diego, 37, 40, 43
    Surrender of Breda by, 37
Venetian painters, 20, 24
Veneziano, Domenico, 20

Venus and Adonis (Rubens), 21, 29
Vermeer, Jan, 34

Water-based painting, 3, 6, 8, 11, 12, 16, 50
    linear quality of, 8, 11
    and oil painting, differences between, 8, 10, 11, 14
    tonality of, 6
White lead priming, 24
Whiting, for water-based gesso, 16

Young Woman Bather (Rembrandt), 28, 34

Library of Congress Cataloging in Publication Data

Fisher, Leonard Everett.
    The art experience.

    SUMMARY: Discusses, with reference to specific paintings, the technique of oil painting and its development over four centuries.
    1. Painting-Juvenile literature. 2. Painting-Technique-Juvenile literature. [1. Painting-Technique] I. Title. II. Title: Oil painting, 15th-19th century.
ND1146.F5   751.4'5   72-5406
ISBN 0-531-02609-4

AUTHOR'S BIOGRAPHY

Leonard Everett Fisher, author-illustrator of the series *Colonial Americans*, and illustrator of some 175 other juvenile works, is widely known in the field of children's literature. In addition, he is a well-recognized painter who devotes much of his time to his art. Born in New York in 1924, he holds Bachelor and Master of Fine Arts degrees from Yale University. He was the 1949 Winchester Fellow in Painting of the Yale School of Fine Arts, a recipient of a Pulitzer painting prize; dean of an art school; president of New England's oldest active art society, The New Haven Paint and Clay Club; and a trustee of the Silvermine Guild of Artists. Well-traveled and having a craftsman's knowledge of painting, and a broad understanding of Western art, he is respected among his painting colleagues as a painter's scholar. As such, he conducts courses in the painter's craft at the Paier and Silvermine Guild Schools of Art in Connecticut. His paintings have been shown over the years in numerous exhibitions including those at such places as the Yale University Art Gallery, the Whitney Museum of American Art, and the Springfield Museum of Fine Art. Manhattan's Hewitt Gallery, the Rochester Institute of Technology, and the Silvermine Guild all have mounted major one-man shows of his work. His paintings have toured nationally under the auspices of the American Federation of Art and the Emily Lowe Foundation. During the late 1940's he was included in several group shows of young painters known as "25 and Under" sponsored by the Seligmann Galleries, New York. Later he was associated with the "Symbolic Realists." More recently, his paintings have been seen in such national shows as "Mainstreams"; the Pennsylvania State University Invitational, "On Living"; Fairfield University's "Artists of Southern New England"; and a number of New England Annuals. In 1970, he completed a wall decoration for a church in Armonk, New York. His art is represented in numerous public collections such as those of the Butler Institute of American Art, Youngstown, Ohio; the Library of Congress, Washington, D.C.; the Norton Gallery of Art, West Palm Beach, Florida; the universities of Oregon, Minnesota, and Fairfield; and the New Haven Paint and Clay Club. Mr. Fisher, his wife Margery, and their three children live in Westport, Connecticut.